Passive Income Lifestyle:

Learn Proven Methods to Make All The Money You Dreamed of With Less Work To Live The Life You Always Wanted

David Vela

Table of Contents

Passive Income 1
Lifestyle: 1
Learn Proven Methods to Make All The Money You Dreamed of With Less Work To Live The Life You Always Wanted 1
What is passive Income 5
Getting in the Right Mindset for Passive Income 8
    Your Dream 8
    Your Plan 9
    Your Fortitude 11
    Advantages of Passive Income 12
    Disadvantages 13
Passive Income Benefits 16
Creative Passive Income Ideas 21
    1. Create a Small Online Course and sell them at Udemy.com 21
    2. YouTube Channel with Residual Income 22
    3. Write for AdSense 26
    4. Selling photos 29
    5. Build an App 30
Investment Passive Income Opportunities 33
    1. Dividend stocks 33
    2. Index funds 34
    3. Investment properties 34
    4. Private Equity Funds 36
    5. REITS 36
Passive Income Ideas for those that Love Selling 38
    1. Designing and Selling T-Shirt with Teespring 38
    2. Amazon FBA 39
The Steps to Using Amazon FBA 41
Affiliate Marketing and How it Helps 44
    What is Affiliate Marketing? 44

How to Market This 45
Steps on how to Affiliate Market for Success 47
Myths about Affiliate Marketing 52
All about Peer-to-Peer Lending 54
What is Peer-to-Peer Lending? 54
The e-book Market 59
Why eBooks?..59
Publishing through Amazon 60
Produce quality...60
Getting New Content Out 61
Keywords 61
Ranking Various Passive Income Streams 63
1) REITS 63
2) Peer-to-Peer Lending (P2P)..63
3) Dividend stocks..64
4) Private Equity Investing 65
5) Creating Your Own Products 66
Warnings about Passive Income 68
Conclusion 72

What is passive Income

This is the first question that many have. Often, this is a question that many feel like they can answer, but they don't have the full definition for it. Well, it's time to learn just what in the world passive income really is, and a bit about what passive income can do for you.
In essence, passive income is a type of income that you don't actively work towards, and not something you're actually working to earn. In many cases, it's also called residual income.

You might wonder what entails this. Well, this can be anything from any money you get from rent, a limited partnership with a company, e-book sales, or even lending and stocks. All of these fall under that umbrella of passive income. These obviously don't include your salary or wage, and there isn't any interest or capital that is gained from this. In many cases, you call this unearned income as well, for it is income that you're not actively working towards.

Now, in contrast, you have active income, which is usually what you're doing right now. It is money that you work towards, and once you stop working, it's not coming in anymore. For example, you work a desk job, you get paid a salary, you quit, you don't get any further money.

This is the same for those that freelance. If you're contracted and you do the work, you'll get paid, if you don't, you won't get paid. It's still active income. Obviously the realm of flexibility is there, but you're not getting money if you stop this.

However, in terms of passive income, you'll get money whether you touch this or not. This might have a lot of work to get started, but once you're starting this, and once you have the passive income stream rolling in, you won't have to make money and keep putting effort there if you don't want to, because it'll keep coming in.

Along with this, you should know that selling a home or stock is not passive income. Because it's in many cases a one-time payment of a large amount, it's still technically active income if you're inheriting stuff, or selling stock or your home. Passive income continues over time. Now if you're looking and buying rental properties and renting them, that residual income is often passive income, whether you're directly working with the place or not. In many cases, the successful ones that use this as a passive income have a property manager that manages this, and you're the higher up that checks in from time to time, but doesn't have to work at this.

Misconceptions of Passive Income

There are a few major misconceptions of this that need to be addressed, for often, people do think about this, and they base many elements off of this. However, it's still important to note that these misconceptions can deter you from where you need to go with this.

The first is that passive income is permanent. No it's not. You might have this going for a while, such as through generations or decades if you're successful, but they do eventually dry up, so don't think this will be there for a kid if you're not putting a tiny bit of effort into this from time to time. If you don't do anything, it will end up drying up.

It also doesn't mean that it's totally secure. It's not. While some forms of income are a lot more trustworthy and secure than others, there is always some risk to it no matter what you do. There is a chance that anything can be destroyed, which is why you create multiple areas of income so you're not making the risk any more than it is.

The biggest one though, is that people think that it's easy and it doesn't take much work. Now there's where the lie is. For many people, this is where they fail, and why some people go belly-up with passive income after a while. It's not easy. Remember, this is life so it's never easy. Making money passively isn't easy. There are some people who like to say that it's easy, but let's face it, it's not. This sort of false hope is why many people will run into this, thinking it's a get-rich-quick scheme, but ultimately it ends up ruining you in the end. The truth of this is that it's hard work and dedication, and you have to put in some extra time and burn the midnight oil when you're beginning this. **We'll go over the logistics of getting started with passive income in the next chapter.**

Passive vs. Semi-Passive

These are two areas that people should learn a bit more about. This will help you understand the differences between both of these.

The first, is passive income. This is the totally passive approach where if you do absolutely nothing to this, you'll get money coming in. Book royalties are a perfect example of this type of income. Regardless of if you do market it like crazy or not, you'll still get people buying your books. You don't have to do a thing to get this income, just deposit any royalties that you have. You don't have to do the dirty work, but it keeps coming in.

Then there is the semi-passive approach, which is something that requires a bit of effort in order to make sure that it's going on. For example, property renting and stock investing is a good example. You need to put in some time and energy in order to do this, such as in the case of property management where you'll need to find tenants, work on the mortgage, insurance, and pay taxes related to this. If you have bad tenants, you'll need to rectify those issues as well. You'll still need to be an employer at some points, so make sure that you do keep this in mind.

This chapter went into depth on what exactly passive income is. It's great to understand the core differences here, because let's face it, many people don't know, and often this is where many fall. Getting the misconceptions out the window before you begin helps too, so you have a clean, fresh outlook on this that will enable you to make the right decisions on what to do here.

Getting in the Right Mindset for Passive Income

Before you can implement any plan to generate passive income, you need to prepare yourself mentally. The good news is that most of these opportunities will cost you nothing or very little money, so you won't be put on hold while you work to make the money to get started. That definitely will come later, but you won't need it to get started. What you do need though is the right mindset to keep you on track.

Your Dream

The primary core of any type of venture has to come from within. We've all had a dream of being an independent person at some point in our lives. Whether we're a child setting up a lemonade stand in front of our house or we're working on a job that is full of drudgery, our thoughts will inevitably drift off to better times.

Think back on your life and try to pull up some of those dreams you've had in the past. The heart of those dreams should serve as the impetus to determining what type of passive income will interest you the most. There are thousands of ways to generate this type of income, but chances are, the methods that will have a better chance of being successful will start with the dreams you have had throughout your life.

For example, if you have always had a dream of writing your own book and making a living as a writer, you should actually follow that spirit. To open up an online store for selling merchandise will likely generate income for you but not likely fuel your inner spirit like writing a book would.

With so many options for creating a passive income for yourself, it is more important than ever that you focus on those dreams that motivate you. Later, as we discuss the different ideas, some will ring true and strike that inner chord to motivate you. Those are the ones you should focus your attention on and will have the best chance of success for you.

Your Plan

Next, you have to start setting some goals for yourself. Start by creating short, medium, and long-term goals. It is okay to say you want to be independent in one year, but you have to set your sites on something a bit more practical. Being financially independent is an ideal goal, but it won't provide you with enough incentive to move forward in your strategy. You need to take your goal-making strategies and take them a step further.

To do that, you need to make smaller and smaller goals. For example, if you want to be financially independent in one year, decide what steps you need to take to accomplish that. You could set up regular milestones perhaps set at 3, 6, and 9 months. When that is finished, take your first milestone at 3 months and break that up into smaller milestones, perhaps three separate goals, one for each month.

Then you could go even further by taking your monthly goal and breaking it up into weekly milestones, then do the same on the weekly basis, and again at the daily basis. Finally, break it down to the 1-day plan, which could be divided up into smaller 1-hour targets.

Now, your plan is broken down into small, bite-sized pieces that are very realistic to follow. This way, your big goal of being financially independent won't seem so far out of reach and will feel like it is very much within your realm of possibilities.

There are a few things you need to keep in mind when you create your goals.

- Each goal must be specific so that you know exactly what you're working for.
- Each goal must be measurable so that you know if you have achieved it.
- Each goal must be achievable so that you know it is possible.
- Each goal must be realistic so that you believe it is within your reach.
- Each goal must have a time frame so that you have boundaries.

To help you recall these guidelines, use the acronym S.M.A.R.T.

Specific

Measurable

Achievable

Realistic

Timed

If each of your goals meets all of these requirements, then you have a plan that is ready to implement.

Your Fortitude

Next, you want to prepare for what others may say or do that could affect your reaching your goals. The idea of generating a passive income is not always appreciated by well-intentioned family members and friends. They may believe that the steps you are about to take are just too risky and try to talk you out of your well-thought-out plan. However, while their words may be tempting, you need to make a commitment to it in order to succeed.

Some people decide to overcome these types of obstacles simply by keeping it a secret and not telling anyone of your plans until they have already achieved some level of success. Others choose to only tell those who are most likely to give them the support they need to help them to accomplish their goals. And some just choose to tell everyone and brace themselves for the fallout. Whatever you choose to do, don't be surprised to find that most people are not willing to join the fun until they see the results for themselves, so you may have to go it alone in the beginning. But remember, this will be a fulfillment of your personal dreams and not theirs so make sure that you only take the advice of someone you want to trade places with.

So, if your dream is to set up your own online dress store, the advice you should listen to should come from someone with a similar dream and drive. Listening to a happy housewife with five kids underfoot will only discourage you. Her dreams and yours are not in alignment; therefore, she will neither understand what you're trying to do and most likely not understand your personal drive to change.

If you're in doubt about any step in your plan, make sure that you ask someone who is capable of not only understanding your business but also your goals. And don't expect everyone in your life to be on board. If you have a question about some avenue of your new venture, always, always, always make sure you ask the right people.

You will make mistakes and you will have setbacks. But rather than have these situations to derail your plans, decide beforehand that you will use each of them as stepping stones to a more successful venture the next time. Rather than let those mistakes defeat you, use them to move you forward, get up, and try again.

As I've said before, this is not a get rich quick scheme nor is it a plan that does not require any work. Passive income requires an investment of time. That is why your detailed plan that we've discussed earlier is so perfect. Because you've divided the job up into smaller, bite-sized pieces, the mistakes that you make in the very beginning will be small and won't cost you as much. But as you master your initial skills, your ability to navigate your plan will improve and you'll be surprised at the strides you'll make.

Advantages of Passive Income

A word of caution is warranted here. The idea of being your own person, free from the encumbrances of a boss dictating your every move can be quite appealing. It is one of the biggest draws for most people seeking a passive income. We've watched them in movies where the whole concept of building your own empire and surpassing that of your boss is beyond desirable. The ability to tell him or her where to "stick it" has crossed the minds of all of us.

Who wouldn't want to get up every morning and walk barefoot from their bedroom to their workspace in their pajamas and flip on the computer to make a few bucks? This is a major advantage of a passive income. You can live and be pretty much anywhere in the world and make your money. So, whether you want to lounge at the beach or climb to the highest mountain peaks, your income will continue to flow in wherever you are.

Another huge advantage that comes from generating a passive income is the free time you will have. In the beginning, you can fully expect that you will do a lot of work, but over time, as your reputation is spread among your potential customer base, you will see that you need to work less and less in order to achieve your goals. Rather than committing all of your time to an employer who wants to pay you only a small payment for the hour, you can dictate when you want to work, how much time you dedicate to any particular project, and exactly when you're ready to walk away.

Once it is all set up, most passive income jobs can run themselves. You won't need to monitor it every minute, and once all the bugs are out of your system, you can simply check in periodically to update it or monitor your strategies as the money rolls in. What you do with all that extra time you have is entirely up to you. There will never be a need for you to get permission to take off for a vacation ever again.

Disadvantages

There are also some disadvantages to a passive income that you need to prepare for. It is not without its own share of work. In essence, you will be starting your own business, which means that you are going to be the sole party responsible for what happens in your business. If you're not accustomed to wearing many hats, this may not be the best choice for you.

Even if you choose to do a job that requires a one-time investment of time, there will always be monitoring and maintenance issues that will have to be dealt with. While we do use the term "passive," do not expect that you won't ever have to dedicate time to keeping your income going. There will always be things you'll have to do in order to keep things running smoothly.

For example, if you do get the income streams you're hoping for, you may have to enlist the aid of an accountant to keep the records straight. No one gets away without having to pay Uncle Sam his due. You'll have to stay in communication with your customers, and you'll need to keep updating the work you've already done; otherwise, your clients may become bored and lose interest. When that happens, you lose money too.

Also, whatever industry you choose to work with, you will definitely need to keep abreast of how it's evolving so that your business will stay in-tune. This means doing additional research and maybe even taking a few classes to keep you competitive.

It won't be passive in the beginning. In fact, it'll be very busy when you first get started. If you're not willing to put in the time up front, there is little chance that you'll produce a steady stream of income later on.

Expect things to happen that are completely out of your realm of control. These could be factors like the economy, the introduction of new technology, lack of buyer interest, or even a new Google algorithm that moves your position around the search engines. To put it simply, a passive income is never guaranteed, and anything can happen to change it, stop it, or just slow it down, and you'll need to change your tactics in order to keep your income going. You may not be able to foresee and prepare for everything, but what you can prepare for is the fact that inevitably things will change and you'll have to have the spirit needed to adapt as time goes on.

Finally, you need some guts; some deep down, intestines of steel guts that will help you to stay the course against all odds. You also need self-discipline in order to keep you on the right track. This is a lesson on passive income, not an I'll get to it when I feel like it income. You may find that you have to do 50- or 60-hour weeks before you can get to the 5-hour week and find time to relax on the beach.

And you can fully expect that if you are successful, you will have to work even harder. There may be many skeptics when you first strike out on your own, but in time, when those same skeptics see your success, you can fully expect them to reemerge as your competitors. Everyone wants a piece of the money pie, but few of them are willing to openly admit it.

Now that you have a pretty good picture of what is expected of you, it is time for you to decide just where you stand on the passive income picture. Many are likely going to step aside, deciding once and for all that this type of work is not for them and that would be fine. It is much better for you to learn and understand this fact before you start and end up sinking a lot of time and money into the venture. However, there will be just as many, if not more, who are even more excited about the possibilities and is ready to jump in with both feet.

Passive Income Benefits

Many people usually make the decision right away after seeing what passive income can do for you, but what if you're not fully sold yet? How do you get on the passive income bandwagon and start working to earn the money that you know you want to earn? Well, how about learning about some of the benefits of this? This chapter will go over some of the amazing benefits of passive income, including what you can get just from switching over to this sort of lifestyle, and encouraging yourself to generate passive income.

More valuable

This is a major benefit of engaging in passive income. In order to be successful with this, you need to have something of value, which essentially means you need to do great work. However, by doing great work, you'll work with greater people, which in turn will add more value to your life.

Often, the biggest complaint many have with their work is that they feel like it's dead-end, not going anywhere, and not of value. Do something valuable with your life, and engage in the passive income opportunity that you've always wanted to have, and something that is certainly of value to your life, and others too.

Forces you to learn new things

This is probably the biggest benefit. Now how many of you can say you know about investing in real estate? Probably not many. For many people out there, forcing yourself to learn new things is something that's a bit crazy. It can be scary, and you'll be worried you screw up.

But learning allows you to understand and get more information about things. Plus, it leads to better income opportunities. Sure, you could stay in your boring job and not continue to learn and grow, but if you engage in passive income, you'll be able to do just that, along with so much more, if you start to take some time and learn new things as well.

You can do other things

You don't just have to get stuck in the tedium of life with passive income. Passive income gives you a chance to work in one venture, but you'll also get to work in other ventures as well. Unlike a conventional job where you're kind of stuck doing the same thing day in and day out, once you're done with one job, you're essentially free to do what you like. This means you can move on and continue to work on a new project, or kick back and reap in what you've sown. Really, it's your choice, and the freedom to do what you want, even in terms of business venture, is what makes passive income so much better than your typical salaried job.

Live wherever you want

You ever wanted to live in your favorite country? Sick of being in the same place? Do you hate the area you live in?

If your answer is yes to any of these, then passive income is your solution.

With rental properties, when you have the establishment set up, you don't have to directly be associated with that. You can check in on them with a conference call once a week, or take a work trip once a year for inspections. You don't have to hang out there all the time, nor do you have to work there.

For many other passive income opportunities, you'll be able to do just that, and so much more. If your goal is to travel the world and see what you've wanted to see, then now is the time to do it, because you can live wherever you want, whenever you want as well.

You're your own boss

You don't have to respond to anyone but yourself, which is both a benefit, and a curse. Some people can't handle this sudden leadership you're given, but this freedom also gives you more chances to do what you want, and make the decisions that you feel right. You'll be able to control the decisions, and people will respond to you.

In contrast, many desk jobs involve you listening to some boss on top, even if you are in a managerial position. If you're sick of doing just that, then it might be time for you to do something about it. Being your own boss is a great thing, and with passive income, you'll get just that.

No company politics

Company politics is something that many people suffer from, even if they don't realize it. Essentially, this is the situation where there are conflicting opinions between yourself and your boss on how to get somewhere on something. This is how arguments happen, and often, the person that seems to be in charge won't let you really do anything, and instead, they tell you basically to shut up, because they're the boss.

Well, if you try to negotiate, that can be hard, and often, they're forced to ignore and do what they want because their boss is the guy in charge. However, when you're working from home, you'll be able to achieve your own goals in your own ways, and you won't have to deal with others. If you're not the type that likes to work with others and dislikes it immensely, then this might be the perfect job for you.

More vacations!

Vacations are something we always yearn for. Walks on the beach, sampling the best food at the fanciest restaurants, all of these are a dream for us. If you're the type who loves to travel the world, or who has yearned for this, but is stuck in a dead-end job because you can't take time off, then it's time to consider passive income.

Passive income allows you to create money needed to do this, but not only that, if you want to take a vacation, you do just that. You run off and take a vacation no matter what people say. If you're the type who wants to explore the world while working, there are chances to do this, and you'll really make a splash in your future by doing just this.

More fun work

Work doesn't have to be boring and tedious. That's a misconception that many people have, and it's something that needs to be nipped in the bud.

For many, they believe that work is all about forcing yourself to work for a menial paycheck, and you have to do something that you hate. But you don't have to do that. If your goal is to be a writer, and you really want to have a publishing business, then is writing and publishing really work? Or is it more fun? **You'll start to realize if you do something you like, the idea of it being a job is less and less of a reality, and it's more of something fun. It's more refreshing, and you'll achieve your goals this way.**

Better Goals

Goals are something that a typical salaried job don't have sadly. Often, when you're working for someone, or at a place, you don't really have an overall goal of where you want to go with this. Essentially, you're just working this as a means to get by, a paycheck for yourself, but what if you could have a goal that you enjoy, and a way to get to it yourself?

Well, passive income gives you this. You'll be able to create your own goals for one, which is something that many people seem less worried about, and not only that, it's a way to have a goal that fits you, and you'll work to it. By having better goals, you'll have more fun, and you'll definitely have a better result from this later on as well.

Higher income Ceiling

Income ceilings are in every salaried jobs you can make money, and you can work all hours of the day, but at the end of the day, that ceiling is always there. You can never make more than what the hourly wage is at the max hours you can do before you go crazy, plus, working 16 hour days is never fun, and not worth the time.

However, with an income ceiling removed, you don't have to do anything, and you'll make a ton of cash. Let's take a rental property. At all hours of the day, you'll be making money, which means you'll be making so much more than you've ever thought possible. By doing this, you'll make a ton more than you expect, and in some cases, people can become millionaires off this alone if they keep at it and have some best property rentals as well.

Better Retirement

Your retirement will be so much better as well. Not only will you have more money to retire with, often, it'll be more than the average pension. Pensions aren't as great as many say, and people still struggle with their bills even after struggling all their lives just to make ends meet before. Do you really want that?

Passive income gives you a chance to save up so much more, giving you a means to really improve your worth later on. By looking at the future, thinking about retirements and all of that, you'll be able to create a better future for yourself and others, something that many don't think about until it's too late.

Creative Passive Income Ideas

Creativity is another great outlet for passive income. After all, it's what helps bring forth new ideas, allowing society to grow. Not only that, creativity is something you can put forward, and if you do this well, you'll be able to really grow in a way. If you're a person with a knack for creativity, then this is one way to do it, and this chapter will go over opportunities you have for passive income in that line of work.

1. Create a Small Online Course and sell them at Udemy.com

Step 1:
Create a short course: You don't need to create an-in-depth online course that cover everything, just a small course with 3 -5 videos and a few worksheets should be find if **you are just starting out.**

Step 2:
Sell it on Udemy.com, because it is a clear winner when it comes to selling online course, it's a very active online learning communities with over 9 million registered students, so the market is there, your job is to research and create a course. (Find a problem that people have and try to solve that problem with an online course).

If you know a lot about a certain sort of subject, this can create a lot of income for you. You'll want to create a course that will help people.

For example, if you know a lot about investing in real estate, or you are good at fishing, writing ... so on, you can create an online course that teach people about that.

Step 3:
In addition to your course, you can also create a membership site where you can constantly add more new contents for your members to learn. You can charge a monthly fee for membership as well.

2. YouTube Channel with Residual Income

YouTube is one of the greatest sites to create a passive income from. For starters, you can create a partnership, where you get money from YouTube for affiliate ads whenever someone clicks on your videos. Google is a lot nicer to YouTube, it puts videos before blogs in many cases on their site. Not only that, people seem more interested in videos than blogs, and videos are much easier to put out.

Do some research on other YouTube channels, what they are doing well, what niches or market they are in, then choose the niche that you are interested in and put together a channel, once you've built it up, you might need to put a new video up every week to keep it going.

How You Can Use YouTube to Create Residual Income

It is totally possible to make money using YouTube, and it can be a great residual income stream. However, it takes a bit to set up, and there are specific steps necessary to generate an income from this. This section will go over the exact steps necessary in order to do this.

1) **Set up your channel:** this is what people will see. You'll first need to have a YouTube account, which is similar to google. You should add keywords to help others find it, and you should make sure that the keywords are relevant to the content that you have as well. You should make a username that is short and catchy, and if you need to, you might want to edit it so it flows better.

2) **Add content:** just start pumping out content, and while it might difficult at first, keep on practicing. You should also ensure that you get better editing software and also a better camera. You should consider using a tripod, getting lighting, and really getting engagement of the product which will in turn get a better audience. Also, it's encourage to upload regularly to help create an audience. If you're regular and maintain a schedule, people will go to it. You should make sure with every video, that you have keywords in the title and the description, which will help drive people to the video from the YouTube search section.

3) **Gain audience**: this is how you increase monetization. You need people to watch the ads that you have before you can make money. There isn't some secret that works fine every time, you just need to create quality content that gets people hooked. You should do uploads regularly and make sure that you are sharing to social media. Distribute it everywhere, and often these subscribers will become partners. You should make sure that you interact with viewers as well, for it will bring more people to the community and make it grow. Plus, they know you're not

just robotically making videos, but you're a person behind it all

4) **Enable monetization:** now before you can earn money, you need to put monetization in, which is essentially giving YouTube the okay to place ads there, and you need to acknowledge that the material isn't copyrighted as well. You just have to click a tab and monetize with ads. Once you upload a video and monetize with ads, you simply go to the video manager and click on the **dollar sign** in order to monetize.

5) **Set up with AdSense:** AdSense is free and you can create an account. You need to be over 18, and you should have a PayPal or bank account with a mailing address and other information to help AdSense figure out who you are and where the money goes. You'll only gain a little bit of money per view, but if you've got an audience, it surely adds up over time. That's why building an audience before you monetize is key.

6) **Check analytics:** once you have the videos up and monetized, and you've got an audience, you should then check out the analytics to find out how they're performing. You can look at earrings, the performance of ads, video views, various demographics and other content.

You should use these tools to see how content resonates with others, and you can change content based on what you find out from this, if you discover some content isn't really fitting for this, or you see that something is doing a whole lot better than other things.

7) **Choose other marketing outlets:** a big thing for those that make videos is they tend to market only on YouTube

and put them there. But remember, blogs can also hold the video there too and you can post it to social media as well. Market it everywhere and get the views that you want from this. If you have more views, you'll be ranked, and people will flock more to it. If you share the link and embed the video, it will also increase the chances of it being seen too, which is super important as well.

8) **Create, create, create:** this is a huge part of it. You shouldn't let the flames go down on creation. Work to create at least one video a week. This is often what many YouTubers do put out each week in order to gain a following. Continue to do this, and do research based on analytics. If for some reason you do have to take a break, you should make sure that your fans know about this. It's often what can make or break a fan base, if you do have personal situations come up, its best to inform them. Remember, they count on you for content, so don't let them down.

9) **Partnership:** this is the final step to really get a lot of money and support. YouTube partnership is essentially various YouTube creators that have monetized videos and a large following. These partners get more content creation tools, and they can often get prizes for the viewers that they have. Partners also get more tips and community support, and this is how many of the major channels have made a lot of money.

For many people, the idea of monetizing on YouTube seems hard. It can be, but these steps showed you just how possible it is, and how you can do it easily, and to a great success and result as well. If you've ever wanted to really get results, try YouTube out, and use these other resources as well to truly create a passive income.

3. Write for AdSense

Essentially, this is writing in very niched subjects for sites such as Squidoo and Yahoo answers. They do differ in how much percentage you get in ad revenue. However, if you put out some good content in such niche areas, it can pay off. You'll get a couple hundred dollars a month for 30 quality articles in the right niches with useful content.

However, if the content is based on the right keywords, you'll get a lot more over time. You can also feel some satisfaction getting money writing some stuff in your spare time. This is good for if you're starting to flex your writing muscles again. If you want to really monetize it, go through product and affiliate links, along with direct advertisements on a blog.

How You Can Write for AdSense

Now, when you're writing for AdSense, you might wonder how you can work with google on this. How can you use your blog or your writing to generate a revenue that you can trust? Well, that's what this section is all about. You can use your website in order to make people buy things. It does take a lot of discipline, but a ton of bloggers can use this. In truth, it actually only takes about four steps, but they are four large steps that do need to be focused on before you do make the profit that you seek to generate.

1) **Determine if eligible:** if you're running a blog, you'll want to make sure that your website follows the guidelines for this, and the program has a specific policy for this. You can look at the AdSense policies that are placed on their site to determine if it's fitting for you.

2) **Increase traffic:** now just because you have a blog that fits, doesn't mean that you're going to be able to whip something up and from there magically get money. You need traffic. You need to know that this runs on a pay-per-click sort of system, which means that you'll only be paid when people click on the advertisements. You'll want to increase the visitors to your website.

There are a few ways to do this. The first, is to get some great high-quality content that is unique. You'll want to ensure that the visitors will go to your blog that has not only unique content that visitors can't find in just about any place, but it also must be of high quality, without errors in both content and the syntax of the words on the page. **If you're creating unique content, it will bring in more people, but the high quality will bring back more of the same.**

You should also make sure that you're using SEO in order to make sure that you're getting the visitors that you want. Ensuring that you have relevant keyword on the title and the actual articles, this will allow you to make sure that your blog will be seen by search engines and shown to the visitors that will look for those keywords.

For example, if your blog post is about learn how to swim, you need to put this keyword: (learn how to swim) in the title and in the blog post.

Finally, promote like crazy. You can do this through social media and social media marketing, or you might team up with another blog that has similar content. You can then comment on other similar blog and link it back to yours. As long as you're not spamming this or doing it excessively, but rather in a professional manner, people will enjoy the content that they get from this in many different ways.

3) **Optimize advertisements:** Adsense will give you a chance to choose which ads you want. You'll be able to display your advertisements along with which colors you have. If you change the location of the advertisements, it

can mean a difference between getting results and none at all.

You should choose a location that isn't super cluttered with anything else, and that looks visually appealing. Often, people like to put them in line with blog posts. You might want to put advertisements below your posts on the blog, which will make them visible but also doesn't take away from the way the design looks. You should also consider putting the advertisements near the left and top of your main page.

According to analytics from Google, this is where you get the most response from advertisements compared to anywhere else. It's probably because it's right there when you see it. Just make sure that it's not conflicting with anything else.

4) **Make sure ads are relevant:** if you're doing a blog on various technology, the last thing you should put on there is home furnishings. With any sort of blog, you should make sure that the content is very relevant. If you're going over the newest video games, you should put ads for various software, keyboards, other accessories, or even game systems and accessories for that. This will get visitors to look at your stuff.

Now, one way to make sure that you're getting your reach that you want and that AdSense gives you the advertisements that you want, is to make sure that your blog is niched and not all over the place. Instead of running a blog for something generic, such as golf clubs, you might want to make sure that its golf clubs for women, where you can go over the newest news about them, along with even reviews and what works best depending on what type of golfer the customer is. And you want to make sure all of the content is relevant, for the more relevant it is, the more ads you'll get that will generate clicks, and it will allow you to get paid.

It's also of note that you can actually get results from this along with others sorts of advertisements. For example, if you want to affiliate market while writing for AdSense, then go for it. Remember, you're working with so many different companies that it's not a problem. You can have it all come from various areas, which is totally fine and actually encouraged. AdSense takes a while to actually build up, but once you do so, you'll end up making more money and getting faster, better results than you have in the past.

4. Selling photos

Step 1:
This is another great one if you're a photographer that has some extra photos here and there. You can **sell them through iStockPhoto, Dreamstime and Shutterstock**. They are free to register and you can start selling right away.

These are the top 3 stock agencies, selling through them is a quick and easy way to get started, because they handle all the marketing side and have large customers base.

Step 2:
Each site has slightly different rules and guidelines and make sure that you take the time to read and understand them.

Step 3:
More promotion: use site like morgufile.com to upload your rejected photos or other photos that you want to give away for free, this gives customer a free sample before they purchase anything from you, this is to build trust and credibility. You need

to create a profile there, then you can add a link to your photos for sale. It's that simple.

You can charge a fee when people download and use your photos. You'll make a bit of residual income each time, and with more photos, the more money you'll make. It's not a ton and shouldn't be put over other options, but it's still a great thing to try if you're looking to really stand out in terms of passive income and the ideas with it.

5. Build an App

This is a passive income that can be super lucrative if you play your cards right. In the age of smartphones, people use apps like crazy. People will download apps for just about anything. It's a great way to make life easier, from putting pictures on a site to even creating photo collages. You might create an app yourself.

There is a lot of competition with this, but remember, creative ideas that are newer can win. If you come up with a unique idea, you'll make money. Simple and yet unique ideas and apps can create passive income. You can hire someone to program and design the apps, which might cost you initially, but the results that you get from this is worth it. You should make sure that you create an app based on your ideas, but also keeping in mind the cost.

Step 1:

Find a problem & research the market: problems are everything, and try to solve that problem by creating an app. You can start by looking for any problems that you have in your daily life, list them out and research if other people have the same problems as well, and try to figure out if you can solve that problems.

To see if there is a demand for the app that you want to create, just go to Google keyword and look for the number of people searching for it. For example, if you want to create an app about teaching other people meditation, just search the keyword (how to meditate) and see how many people are searching for that, if there are a lot of demand, this means that it's viable to go and create an app.

Step 2:
Start brainstorm the flow and features of your app: write them down on paper, what will the app do to help the users solve their problems, and how the users can quickly and easily navigate the app.

Step 3:
Hire a designer/developer to create your app, you can go to Upwork.com, freelancer.com or odesk.com, make sure to check their credibility and their portfolio before you work with them. And one thing I want to mention here is, don't just choose the one with the lowest price, and don't go with the highest one as well. Choose the medium one.

Step 4:
Create your developer accounts with varies app stores and start selling there, make sure you read and understand their terms and conditions.

Step 5:
Integrate analytics, this helps you understand user engagement and retention of the app. Once your app is lived, you will start getting feedbacks from users, this will allow you to make improvements and add features to the app, and make even better.

Investment Passive Income Opportunities

Investments is one of the first outlets many people will turn to when it comes to passive income. There are some great investment chances out there for you to choose from. Not only that, investments do add up over time, and often, if you sell or cash in on an investment, but then try once more, you'll be able to net further benefits from this. This chapter will go over how investment passive income opportunities work, and how you can really benefit from

1. Dividend stocks

This is the first, and one of the easiest ways to create a passive income. Essentially, what you're doing is you're getting paid to own a stock, which is a share of the company. As the company earns money, part of it is put to the side and paid to the investors.

For example, let's say that you own stock in a popular fast food chain. When the company rakes in some money, part of that goes to you if you have a bit of a stake in it. Now this money can then be reinvested in more stocks and shares if you like, which could then lead you to more money, or you back out now and receive a cash payment.

The yields for this can vary greatly from one company to the next and they can fluctuate. If you're unsure about how to do this, you should go with one that is a dividend aristocrat, which is one that has been growing over the last 25 years.

One thing to note about stocks is that you'll want to learn the market and the market trends. This can be simple with smaller shares in large companies that will obviously increase, but it can be risky. Sometimes the market trends might predict a downfall you're not really seeing until it's too late. Do some research on stocks and how to invest in the stock market. It's one of the easiest investment means and it's much simpler than other stock trade options, so it might be what works best for you.

2. *Index funds*

Index funds are essentially mutual funds that are part of a certain market, which will mirror the performance of the index that they track, and they'll be advantageous in many ways over other investments who want to have passive income. Index funds are diversified which is good for investors, instead of just buying a few stocks, you are now buying different stocks from a lot of different companies.

These funds are typically passively managed and they don't have anything change unless the actual index changes, which for investors means less work, and you just have to check in every now and then.

3. *Investment properties*

This is the first and most major means to create a passive income that is successful. To put it into perspective, 10 real estate properties that will get you $420 a month each will total over 50 grand each year. Now that's just ten little ones. Let's say you own a complex with apartments. This can net you a ton of money, and in essence, once you learn the game, you'll know what to do, and is really the best way for some who want to get into passive income and are willing to learn will want to do.

Now, the first thing you'll want to do is learn the playing field. Real estate requires a lot of homework, and you'll want to make sure that you're interested in this before you begin. You should from this, create your own path and create a risk tolerance in order to achieve this.

Some people do like to crowdfund these initially, others like to save money over time to do this, but the main thing you want to do is generate enough income to purchase a real estate property, and from there work to improve it over time. However, by doing it through a crowdfunding area such as RealityShares, you'll be able to help get support from others. You'll be able to link some of your money to this as well, and from there, you'll get the others helping to invest.

Now once you have the money, this is where the fun begins. You start by looking for the right place. Look for hot areas, areas that have decent neighborhoods, and places that'll sell or get renters. Look at the market and determine the correct area. Work with the real estate agent to buy the property, and then get someone into there.

When looking for those to invest, you want someone that you can trust. You don't want someone that doesn't pay their rent on time, or they create messes. You also don't want someone that won't give you the information you need. Rather, look for someone you can trust.

Then, you just collect the money and then move to your next property. Once you have a few secured, you can sit back and relax, or you can then improve further properties. You can then move to purchasing multifamily homes, where more than one family lives there, and as their landlord, you're taking care of this.

You can also do apartments, which require more money and work, but you can hire others to take care of that. You'll just have to do some housekeeping endeavors and collect some checks once you're ready to move forward.

Now, it's imperative that when you get started with real estate investing, you do your homework, not just on what to do right, but what could go wrong. Lots of things can happen, and often, these properties can come with some costly, high-effort problems that are often unexpected, so you should be ready to face those when you can, because they're just as important as the little things as well.

Before you get into this one, it's important you really get the knowledge necessary to handle this. Read from other investors, do your homework, but most of all make the decision yourself on whether or not you want to do this, and you'll be able to definitely do well with this.

4. Private Equity Funds

This is another form of real estate investing which is essentially a collective fund that takes money from many investors and then puts it in real estate. Often, these have a lot of different people in it, which creates a diversification in this, and often, this is very rigorous in many cases, especially for underwriters.

These private equity fund investments aren't illiquid though, and they can carry high investment mediums. Often, these are formed by investors with a high worth, with a 2% fee that happens every single year, plus 20% of all profits earned. It's a good means to get started, but just know it is pricy as well.

5. REITS

These are real estate investment trusts, which are essentially large portfolios of income real estate. With REITs, t's a powerful way to invest in real estate then privately owing building. Often, REITs need to distribute 90% of their earnings each year. The income comes from rent, leasing of the properties and more.

Now, this source of investment does require strict compliance standards, but also this means that there is a higher quality for the investment strategy and the real estate experience.

Often, there are two types of people who are into this: traded and not traded. Now, a traded REIT gives you the chance to be traded openly, which gives and investor more liquidity. However, this is likely priced into the value of this, which creates a premium and lower relative returns, regardless of whether or not you choose your share. Along with this, they tend to have a higher volatility in the market, which means that they can fluctuate in one way or another depending on how the market is, regardless of you directly changing it or not, or even how the property changes.

However, these are very popular because of how large the dividends is. Often, the non-traded ones are under scrutiny because of the upfront fees that get charged, and also the dubious practices associated with this. **That's something to keep in mind if you're considering a chance to invest in that means.**

Passive Income Ideas for those that Love Selling

Now, for those that love to sell things, this is such a great means to create a passive income. With Amazon FBA and other opportunities out there, having some ways to really make things go right with selling do make it even better. If you're a fan of selling stuff online, then this is for you.

1. Designing and Selling T-Shirt with Teespring

Now many people are buying their clothing online, this is the perfect time to get into this business. Teespring is a platform for custom apparel, you can upload your t-shirt design and start selling there in minutes.

Step 1:
Design your shirt: you can hire someone to design your t-shirt for you and upload that to Teespring. Or you can do it yourself by using their online tool, they have extensive library of clipart and font to choose from.

Step 2:
 You need to set the price of your t-shirt, and then set your sales goal, sale goal is the minimum number of t-shirt that you need to sell before they can print the t-shirt. It can be anything from 5 – 1000, the higher your sale goal, the more money you will make per sale. I normally set my sale goal to 10.

Step 3:
Set up your campaign: come up with a good title and description for your t-shirt campaign and set your duration of the campaign running, it can be 3 – 21 days.

Step 4:
Promotion: this can be done through varies ways, like telling family and friends on Facebook about your t-shirt so they can help your spread the words, or using Facebook ads to promote your t-shirt.

Step 5:
When you reach your sales goal, for example: 10 t-shirts, Teespring will print and mail the shirt to your customers and pay you via PayPal.

2. *Amazon FBA*

If you're looking for a way to get a ton of products and then have them get handled directly by amazon, you totally can. Amazon FBA is a lifesaver for many that are looking to sell on Amazon.

Essentially, Amazon FBA handles the entire nitty-gritty of the transaction, you just have to list the product. What you do, is you send them the product, and they sort them into various categories. When it sells, they handle the rest and get the product to the customer. It's that simple.

Now, when you're looking to sell a lot of one thing, such as buying something in bulk and listing it, this can be a lifesaver. For those looking to engage in the passive income of reselling products in bulk, this is how you do it. You leave it with them, it sells, and they do the rest. You don't have to do anything with this, and it's something that you'll definitely get a lot of benefits from.

With Amazon FBA, you only have to give them a percentage of the sales. This is something that can passively grow over time. You don't even have to have the products yourself. You can pay in bulk and send it there.

Amazon FBA is a great way to generate passive income for many reasons. For one, it's super simple to do this. You just need to check and list products, you then just have to make sure that you keep the stock high, and reorder when necessary.

Not only that, it can save you a lot of money on postage. With many people, postage is something that can rack up, but amazon calculates all of that into the transaction, and in many cases is faster due to two-day shipping. Amazon FBA allows you to do something about this, without putting the effort forward.

Finally, Amazon FBA is great if you're looking to do this for the long run. Yes, it'll be pricy initially, just like all passive income opportunities, but the results from this are more than worth it, you just need to put the time in. Compared to other passive income strategies, you'll definitely need to put less time in, and it is easier, you just have to keep at it.

You'll want to have something that will stand out. Make sure that the pricing is both decent, but also competitive as well. You shouldn't let it be too high, but also not too low that it won't make a profit. That's something to definitely keep in mind. Make sure it's something that will sell too. Sure, there might be something that nets a bulk of profit, but if it's not selling, then what in the world is the point of getting it?

The Steps to Using Amazon FBA

Amazon FBA is relatively simple, and you'll be able to do it in these six simple steps. They are as follows:

1) **Send your inventory:** you will be using their carrier system to get your products there. Typically the Amazon FBA system works with you, and you need to simply print out the packaging and send it out to them. You'll need to go to your Seller Central account and choose Amazon FBA from the tab in order to use this.

   Typically this is best used with a professional account, since it does take away a chunk of your money, so you'll want to ensure you're selling before you use this.

2) **Receive and store:** amazon will receive the product and they will place it in a central area. You'll have the opportunity now to list the product.

3) **List product and get customers in:** to do this, you simply list the product and get the customer interest. Use keywords to help narrow down the searches, giving a great description and a catchy title to help lure people in. it's imperative that you use keyword, since it help with getting ranking on Amazon's site. The customer will then choose the product and it'll then be purchased. Some of these do come with free shipping, and with Amazon FBA, more often than not people use prime to get this.

4) **Pick and ship:** this is Amazon's job. Typically, they will pack everything and pick it from where your inventory is. They'll then ship it out to the customer.

5) **Customer service:** this is another aspect Amazon helps with. If a customer isn't satisfied, amazon will step in to assist you with this, and they have a 24/7 response team that will allow you to get inquiries and complaints satisfied via their customer service if something is wrong.

6) **Continue to list and ship:** at this point, amazon handless the dirty work, you just need to get the products out there to them, and you'll want to ensure that they're there for them to pick and ship. If you run out of stock, get some new ones. This is a key point on your part, **because if they don't have anything and a customer buys it, it falls on you, simply because they will complain.**

Now one of the good things about Amazon FBA is that often, the ones that you'll be putting up there are those that are eligible for prime, which is a great way to get rankings. If you want people to actually buy your stuff, ensure that it is prime eligible.

Most of the people who shop on Amazon are prime shoppers, and often using FBA will give you a higher discovery, because if there is prime shipping, it gets people more inspired to buy it, and often, these prime filtered searches do appear more than your traditional searches. Plus, the prime users increase with the seasonal times, and they do get a huge boost during the holidays. You'll also get a way better conversion if you do use prime eligible on your products, and this will inevitably increase your sales.

The Cost

There is one downfall to this which was touched on earlier, and that is the cost. Now, when you sell on Amazon, you get charged a percentage of the product that you're selling. However, with Amazon FBA, it's a bit more, based on the following factors: fees for handling, the square footage of storage and their costs, the weight of the item, and also the fee to pick and pack this. This is often not considered, but think about it, the people that are working at these amazon facilities need to be paid for this work, and often, it's something that people forget, but while it can be expensive for some, it does take into consideration all the fees for this.

FBA is a good investment if you're having an increase of volume and exposure. For example, let's say that you have an online clothing boutique, and people are buying left and right. You can't keep up with the postage, orders, and the like, and it's taking up way too much space in your home or public storage. This is when you start to consider Amazon FBA. FBA is a great investment at this point, and it definitely does help with bulk sales.

If your clothing store for example does go FBA, sure you might make less per sale because of that, but if you're selling so many that it won't make a difference and it'll actually help you instead of making you scramble to ship 500 items a day (a bit of an exaggeration but you get the picture).

Affiliate Marketing and How it Helps

Affiliate marketing is another source of passive income. Now, if you're the type who has a website, or you've always wanted one to really generate the best passive income that you can, this is for you. Affiliate marketing is one of the best ways to create a great source of passive income, and this chapter will go over the ins and outs of it, including what you need to do to start, along with some help on how to really springboard your ability to do this to a new level.

What is Affiliate Marketing?

You might wonder initially what in the world affiliate marketing is. Well to start, it's where most people get started with passive income, and it's something that many people can enjoy.

The main theory behind this is essentially you take the time to promote people's products, which in turn will get you a commission from each sale from all of your marketing.

Really, the main focal point of this if revenue sharing. Let's take for example a company that has this new best product. Sure, they could do all their marketing by themselves, but what if they could pay a nominal fee to every single person that helps sell a product, and thus getting the word out further and further to everyone? That's the theory behind this. If you don't have a product and you want to make money from this, essentially you can grab some product that fits whatever you want to market and you'll get an income from it.

Now, let's go over the theory behind this. There are three spheres of influence that entail the idea of affiliate marketing. **They are**

the merchant that sells this, the publisher, and the customer.

The merchant is the one that creates the product. Let's say that you're wanting to affiliate market vacuum cleaners, the ones that do sell the cleaners and have created it are the merchants. These are the ones people go to in order to buy.

The publisher is the affiliate marketer themselves. In this, they put ads up everywhere, or even create articles in order to sell these products. They take what these merchants have, and create content that get people to buy this. A popular example is going to thisiswhyimbroke.com which showcases various awesome products. You might read a small review on the product, and then, you see the link to buy it below. As the publisher, that's where the people will go to the merchant, and get it. The merchant sees they got the sale from your site, and then, you get the commission.

Finally, there's the customer, the one who reads the article, sees this sweet new product and goes "wow, I could totally use that!" and they then buy it from the merchant. **This is the public you're going for, and it's something that definitely works.**

How to Market This

Often, there are different ways to market these types of affiliate marketing. For example, you've probably seen review sites that go over these various products from one seller, and from there the person can then choose to get one product or not. This is a great way to do it.

Another great example is an entire website dedicated to niche stuff. Say for example, you really like retro game memorabilia, so you create an entire website about that, including retro products that people might like, such as old video game jewelry and the like. You then write a description or review to sell the person, and then, you create an affiliate link for them to get it. This is one of the best ways to do it, and you'll definitely see this working as well.

Now, with affiliate marketing, there is something that won't work. This is banner ads. Let's face it, banner ads look so tacky it hurts, and often, people like to ignore them, or worse, Ad Block pushes those ads out from view. You're not going to get anything from people if you use that. Simple as that.

However, you can be clever with the way you affiliate link. One of the best ways is to put in some keywords linking to this, or even a link to the product at the end. You can kind of tell others in a sense that you're an affiliate marketer from this, but in many cases, people don't even know that's the system unless they actually do research on affiliate marketing, so you can definitely get a result from this.

When it comes to affiliate marketing, you have to have the right ads, so look at your site, and choose ones that fit.

Steps on how to Affiliate Market for Success

Now, you might wonder where to begin, or even what to do with this. Well, there are some exact steps you can take in order to become an affiliate marketer, and this section will give you the how-to in order to do this:

1) **Choose who to become an affiliate for:** this is very important. It's imperative that you start affiliating with a niche that fits you. For example, if you're an interior designer or know a lot about it, you'd sell household goods, not pest control sprays and such. You want to sell what you know, for it makes the next few steps so much easier.

2) **Start a website:** before you begin to affiliate, you should first create a website. This is because the companies want to ensure that you have a website that fits them. You shouldn't make the content extremely in tune with sales, but instead make it about the niche more than anything. If you're struggling with starting a site, go to **WordPress.com** to get some help in skyrocketing this.

3) **Do your research:** not all affiliate programs are fitting to your niche. It's important to make sure that you do choose ones that fit.

    For example, if you're wanting to include products that you might see on a site in order to sell, you might choose Amazon. This is good if you're beginning with products.

    There is also other affiliate network such as **Commission Junction**, which gives you a chance to become an affiliate for many companies that might have a whole array of products, such as Overstock, Office Depot, and other relevant sites.

Clickbank is a great one to start out with too because it does give you commissions from companies that can be lucrative to niche sites. Whatever you choose though, figure out the program that best fits the niche of your site.

4) **Join an affiliate program:** once you find the right one, it's time to join. Now, it's free to join, but if there is a place asking for credit card information, you might be getting scammed. Most affiliate programs are free, so keep an eye out for that. there are options for PayPal though, however, it's not because they want to scam you, but it's how they pay for the commission, so make sure you don't freak out if you see that.

5) **Adding affiliate links:** now once you have the affiliate partnership is to put in affiliate links. This is a way to get a paid commission without outright telling people you're an affiliate marketer. They can simply click the link, and you'll get the commission. For example, if you're writing about landscape paintings, you can affiliate link to Amazon where it shows landscape pictures only. This will give people a chance to go through the site and get some items. It's very easy to get links for sites too, which is pretty amazing.

6) **Visual ads:** now banner ads are not as great as actual link ads, but if you want to give people more options, you can put some visual ads on the sidebar for the niche that you're writing in. companies make this easy to put on sites, so you can get the images and links to bring people there, so you just need to make a simply copy/paste in order to ensure that people can see the sidebar ads and go through with the purchase.

7) **Create content:** this is very important for some affiliates. They sometimes forget that the site is what matters, not just the links to selling stuff. This will create more traffic to the site, so you should create more content. This gets people coming back to the site, and is often called **content marketing.** Along with this as well, with the more content that you put up, the more links. This will give more chances to lure people to these sites, allowing you to get even more commission from this. Content is so important to sites, and it often goes by the boards in many cases. Don't do this to the site and instead continue to cultivate it.

8) **Check out the analytics:** analytics are essentially the information that tells you whether something is selling, how it was sold, and who you sold it too. You'll be able to use these analytics to tell you what's working or not. For example, if you notice that one product is totally kicking butt on your site, then by all means continue to promote that. You should take a look at your demographics too, and tailor the content to that demographic. Recent visitors are also important, especially since if you see more people flocking to one over the other, it might be great to put more affiliate links there. Most of all, look at what works and what doesn't work, for it will tell you what's working and what's not. Keep what's working in place and get rid of what isn't working.

9) **Keep promoting:** you are at the point when you're doing this to decide whether you want to keep expending or not. If you choose the latter, it will contract the business, however with the former, it will give you more money. You should choose to expand by making sure that you do include new products when the time is right. If you see a product that's totally fitting for this, you should seek to market this. If you want to look for other sites, that's totally fine. You should also make sure that you never

stop promoting. Always promote on social media when you can, and do other types of marketing to get people to your site to increase traffic.

10) **Delegate tasks:** once your business expands, you should make sure that you do take care of growing your business by getting others to help you. Yes, it might cost you a bit, but this is indeed an investment that will allow you to improve your affiliate business. It will also give you more time to focus on expansion, a major part of affiliate marketing and those tasks.

11) **Automate:** now, this is a step that many people tend to forget. Automating is there, and there are a lot of various digital marketing tools that you can use to help you improve this. You'll probably need to put some money into this because it can be an investment, but it will give you extra time, and when you decide to let this become passive, you'll be able to reap the returns on investments with this. You should focus on creating a strategy for your business while you have these tools in place and the employees to continue the daily tasks. This will free you up to handle the big picture and give you a chance to grow.

12) When you're doing this, always make sure that you come back to the bigger picture to ensure that you're on the right track. Sometimes people get focused on the here and now that they don't really focus on the future. Yes, there are some things that you can do in order to make it easier at that time, but don't forget the big goal that you have there, **which is a passive income.**

These steps are what you should take in order to be successful in affiliate marketing. The biggest part is really building the website and maintaining this, so I suggest to get some practice in that first before you continue on. With that in mind, it'll allow you to get a better sort of look at what you should do next, and allow you to perfect the site so that it gives you good content.

By using these types of selling passive income strategies, you'll be able to create the best sort of passive income lifestyle you want. Selling things online is really the new thing these days, and while owning properties and such might be good for those looking for a bigger sort of investment, if you don't have the time or the money to be doing that at the moment, and while you're working to create a stable job, this could be the break you've been looking for. Selling is fun, and once it becomes passive, you can make some serious cash with this as well.

Myths about Affiliate Marketing

Shockingly enough, there is a lot of hearsay about affiliate marketing that many people don't realize is just not true. However, it's imperative to know about this, because if you don't, you could end up wrecking your system, and making your website look bad. This section will talk about the myths you need to know when it comes to affiliate marketing.

The first, is that affiliate marketing is quick to grow and easy to manage. It's not. You need to have a website that's been doing relatively well, but gets good traffic for it to actually generate any sort of income from this. You need to ensure that you keep the website going, along with putting affiliate links here and there. Very few have been in it for a long time as well, so it's important to remember that you might not get results right away, just like any other passive marketing technique.

The second, is that you need to be super niche and totally popular. This is a bit true, but not as true as you think. Some might get into deeper niches even if they don't really like the niche because they think it's where they need to go. However, while it is important that many of the popular niches do well, you'll still have success. As long as you keep it aligned with your site in general and have fitting affiliates, you'll be able to create a better and working market.

The third, is that affiliate marketing doesn't work with SEO anymore. That's not really the case. While the new algorithms are making link building outdated and making people not want to affiliate market, there are ways to use SEO to create a brand. With new keyword and other such means, you can still get affiliate results from your website. You might have some link problems with google if you're not managing this well, but most of the time you're still able to use affiliate marketing with google, giving you a chance to still give relevant information to others. So don't let the new SEO changes scare you away, but instead, keep it going and work with the system, bettering this over time as well.

The fourth and final sort of myth that many think about is that they believe you have to have a ton of affiliate links on your website, or get as many sites with products on there as you can. However, **this is where the quality notion comes in**. There are tons of affiliate programs out there, and you might think you need to sandbag them all. But that's not the case. What you need to do here is simple, find the right affiliate programs that best fit your site, and you'll want to see good products that will be fitting. You shouldn't keep various affiliates that aren't generating revenue as you start to grow. In essence, if you keep affiliate merchants that fit your brand, and not just any old one, it'll give you results. You will want to get the right sorts of merchants that do deliver results.

Now that you know about affiliate marketing, you'll realize that yes, it isn't easy. Nothing comes easy in life, and this does take work. But once you realize this, and come to terms with this, you'll be able to create a better, more rewarding business because of this, and you'll generate the passive income that you know you need.

All about Peer-to-Peer Lending

Peer-to-peer lending is another passive income source that might be interesting. Now, if you have money, or maybe wants to lend to others and get a lot back, this is for you. Now **it's important to note that there is risk associated with this**, so be mindful before you begin. We'll go into further detail on these risks, including what might happen and how you can avoid this.

What is Peer-to-Peer Lending?

You might wonder how in the world a lending site would even work to create passive income. Well, as of late, this has become popular, and in a sense, this is a sort of "crowd lending." Now, this might be something you raise an eyebrow at, because how can you trust someone to give you money back, when many of us actually don't even get that from our close friends? Well, here's how.

These are all protected by sites, and often, this is where people will look for personal loans, and it's a way for people with unfavorable credit to get the money that they need. Essentially, these people that come here need a loan, such as to help with a business, get out of debt, money for a home, or something like that. They then sign up for a loan, and then, they become a borrower.

Now you're an investor at this point, and in essence, you're basically the bank. You're giving these people your own money, and once it's lent, the borrower must give it back to the investors within a time limit, and with an interest rate. The lending site does take a small percentage on a loan, which is essentially the brokering fee for the business transaction.

You saw the word interest in this, and this is how you'll make money. Each loan does have a small interest attached to this that is charged like how a loan from your local bank might have. The interest really depends on the credit rating, and for those that have good credit pay lower interest rates, but with bad credit the interest rate is higher.

Now this is how the investor comes in. Most of these people can borrow up to 30 grand or so from the site, and these maturities on the loans can be up to five years, and the interest rates are based off the credit card criteria to give you the best buyers. For an investor, you can definitely make a ton of money from this, and often, **you'll be able to if you're smart with choosing buyers, which we'll get into later.**

Now, because of how high the interest rates can go, even as great as 30%. They are higher than other bonds and have less risks, many investors will sponsor loans and hope they'll get some returns. Often, these returns average between 5-12%. With various other streams, this can end up being a ton of money. This is a great alternative to investments, and if you're not keen on using the stock market fluctuations as a way to generate money, then this is the way to do it, and you'll get consistent and very steady returns.

Best Sites for this

Now going through the right site is the one key thing to keep in mind. This section will highlight a few sites to check out, along with why they're considered the best in the business.

> **Upstart:** this is a peer-to-peer lending site that was found by two googlers. The loan eligibility for this goes past the FICO score, and they base this on academic performance, and even work history. You can typically have loans that go from 3K-35K, with an APR of 4.7%, which is more than most banks. People will use this to buy cars, pay off loans,

or even help with starting the business. It typically attracts younger buyers

Funding circle: this is a marketplace for small business loans in the US and UK. Typically, this is used to facilitate small business funding, since typically it's very hard for the traditional banking system to help with business. After one loan was rejected too many times by one of the founders, they created this for small business owners. Right now it currently works with over 40K retail investors. Often, these loans are much higher, going from 25K-500K, **which might not be good for starting investors unless you have money.** The business has a five-year tenure on the loans as well. This is good if you have more money and are willing to take a larger risk.

Prosper marketplace: this is the first P2P lending site in the US. It has over 250K people on it, and has funded over $4 billion in various types of loans. You can have loans that work with debt consolidation, loan improvement, vehicle loans, small business loans, and even engagement ring loans. These loans minimally are from 2K-35K for most people, and the APR is from 5.99% depending on what type of buyer you have. **Often, these lenders don't have to put in much, as little as 25 dollars per note, and these come with great returns and a cash flow option as well. This is one of the key sites for those starting out, especially if you're not super ready to invest a ton of money as of yet.**

A Few Cautions

Now we went over how you're working with buyers, and while there are great ones out there, in this sort of lending, you've got to do your homework. **Now, the one thing you shouldn't do in this, is just invest a lump sum into one person,** especially if it's all of this. The reason being, is while that borrower might have been great once in the past, people's lives change, and they end up royally screwing other people over, and this is how incidents such as people losing investments happen. You don' want this, so there are a few things that you'll want to do.

When you start, you shouldn't put everything into one person, what you should do, is **put a bit into many people.** Now, this can be as low as 25 dollar notes. You can have that as a portion of the loan, and you'll be able to get some money from each stream. Let's say you purchase 2500 dollars' worth of notes. Essentially, that's 100 of them, and you're spreading the wealth to 100 different lenders. Now, let's say a few of them flake out, but you get about 90 of these back, with the interest rates in hand, you'll be able to get a profit from this even with the people flaking out. In contrast, those that lend to one person and get burned end up losing everything on one person. You should make sure to look at the risks as well, and you'll see the cash flow grow.

The second thing that you should worry about is the type of borrower that you want. Now, sometimes borrowers do default, and that means they can't pay it back. When this happens, the P2P site will try to get the borrower in claims to give the money back that they owe. Now because this unsecured, it's often just lost.

Because of this, when you're a lender, you need to look at the credit that this person has. It's not enough just to look at the score. While that does help, you'll want to make sure that they have a good lending history as well. Now, despite the fact that the ones with the highest credit have the lowest returns, it's often the least amount of risk, and you will profit from this, which is why this takes a bit to take off. If you get someone with low credit, they won't meet the obligations, and you'll start to lose money. Essentially, do as much of a background check as possible on every single lender before you give your money out, and definitely consider spreading your money to many people, because this can definitely save your bacon over time.

Peer-to-peer lending sounds dubious when you hear about it initially, but once you start to do your research, you'll realize it's just as great of a passive income stream as any other. Try it, and you may never be the same.

The e-book Market

This is one of the most popular, and really the easiest for many, sources of passive income. However, because it is easy and one of the most popular, it can be hard to stand out from the crowd. But there are means to do this, ways to really make yourself stand forward and proud, inciting interest from others on what you're selling. This chapter will give you further details on what the e-book market is, and how to be successful with this.

Why eBooks?

You might wonder why you should look at eBooks, and if you're someone that likes to write, but has never really published anything, it might seem like something crazy. Well, think about it, with the changes of the eBook industry along with self-publishing, it's possible for regular people to write books on anything, and even get a passive income. Some people make thousands of dollars just from this. One person even made 65 grand in eBook publishing for a month. It's a ton of revenue, and it's great.

Now, one great thing about this, is that it's super cheap. You don't even have to write or be an expert in what you want to put together. You should at least have a great draft, a good editor, and someone who can make your eBook shine and stand out. EBook publishing is super simple now, and you can even do it through amazon.

Now, some might wonder why you would do this over traditional publishing. It's simple: less gatekeepers. If you want to get something published, good luck getting it through the first fifty publishing houses. By doing it yourself, you can market it, and you'll be able to earn a residual income.

Publishing through Amazon

Amazon is the best digital publisher. For starters, everyone knows about it, and there are thousands of people downloading every day. Some might believe selling on other sites works, but in truth, you'll not get as much of a result. For a successful book, you can get almost 700-1000 downloads, which is thousands every month in income.

It's also made simple as well. Amazon now has kindle direct publishing, where you put digital books onto the site with no fee attached to it. When you do this, you get 35-70% of the sales price depending on if you do it through the KDP or KDP select. Essentially, KDP uses the .mobi sort of formatting for this, for it looks better because all tables and images are intact. You can get the conversion software through Calibre. You can also pay someone to format this for you as well.

Now, it was discussed about KDP select. By doing this, you get true marketing. You give them an exclusive sort of selection on your book for 90 days, and you get higher royalties, and you're part of the lending library. You then get a percentage of total members. It can also be discounted or free as well for a few days to get the downloads. **Simply put, amazon is the best powerhouse if you want to eBook publish.**

Produce quality

One big thing to remember is you want quality. Now because anyone can publish what they want, there's a lot of bad books out there, and that can deter people from coming back. You should make sure that you do put out great content that does help people, it will get you better and higher reviews, which in turn will get more sales.

This will also build a following, which will give you more sales. People will want to follow you. This is why quality matters, since people will come back for more.

Getting New Content Out

Because of the fact that there is so much, you'll want to get a lot out. People will come to you after they read a good book and they'll want more. If you don't have more, there will be disappointment, for they might move onto something else. Nobody gets rich with one book, **but rather, you need a portfolio of various types of books out there,** which will give you more control over the subject. You'll get more money, and definitely more sales and a bigger following.

If you are going to put out a series of book, make sure that the subject matter fits each one, especially if you want to capitalize on the audience you have. For example, don't write a book on investing, and then try to get people to buy a book on crocheting. Chances are, they won't convert.

Keywords

Keyword is another key part. Many forget that amazon is a search engine, which will give the users what they are looking for, which then will give you products that are relevant. This is why you should ensure that you have keywords in the book title and description, you'll get a lot more results from those that search. You'll try to go for niche sort of keywords as well.

Book publishing is something that does take time, patience, and a knack for quality content. However, if you do just this, keeping in mind these various parts, you'll certainly get the results you hope to achieve. In the world of book publishing, it is a surefire way to get a passive income going.

Ranking Various Passive Income Streams

Below are the main passive income investments to consider. Each passive income stream will be ranked based on Risk and Return. We rank starting from the most capital intensive idea and one that takes time to break even to the least capital investment and easy to start ideas.

1) REITS

For those willing to take on the task of managing a property, real estate can be a powerful semi-passive income stream due to the combination of rental and principal value appreciation. But to generate passive income from real estate, you either have to rent out a room in your house, rent out your entire house and rent elsewhere (seems counterproductive), or buy a rental property. It's important to realize that owning your primary residence means you are neutral the real estate market. Renting means you are short the real estate market, and only after buying two or more properties are you actually long real estate.

In order to generate $10,000 in Net Operating Profit After Tax (NOPAT) through a rental property, you must own a $50,000 property with an unheard of 20% net rental yield, a $100,000 property with a rare 10% net rental yield, or a more realistic $200,000 property with a 5% net rental yield. When I say net rental yield, I'm talking about rental income minus all expenses, including a mortgage, operating expenses, insurance, and property taxes.

2) *Peer-to-Peer Lending (P2P)*

P2P lending started in San Francisco with Lending Club in mid-2000. The idea of peer-to-peer lending is to disintermediate banks and help denied borrowers get loans at potentially lower rates compared to the rates of larger financial institutions. What was once a very nascent industry has now grown into a multi-billion dollar business with full regulation.

Lending Club went public in 2014 and is now worth about $1.7B. They advertise P2P lending returns of over 7% for well-diversified portfolios of over 100 notes. I've personally been able to achieve a 7.4% annual return over the past two years in a completely passive way by investing in A and AA notes. Others have achieved a 10% annual return through relatively minimum effort.

To achieve $10,000 in annual passive income through P2P at a 7% rate, you need to invest $142,800 in hundreds of high-grade notes. The higher the interest rate, the higher the risk. P2P lending has taken me the longest to get comfortable with because I really dislike the idea of people not paying me back (breaking their honor.

3) Dividend stocks

Investing in large cap dividend companies is one of the best ways to build passive income. The "Dividend Aristocrats" are a list of blue chip companies in the S&P 500 that have demonstrated a consistent increase in dividend payouts over the years.
Let's say a company earns $1 a share and pays out 75 cents in the form of a dividend. That's a 75% dividend payout ratio. Let's say the next year the company earns $2 a share and pays out $1 in the form of dividends. Although the dividend payout ratio declines to 50%, due the company wanting to spend more CAPEX on expansion, at least the absolute dividend amount increases.

Dividend stocks tend to be more mature companies that are past their high growth stage. Utilities, telecoms, and financial sectors tend to make up the majority of dividend paying companies. Tech, Internet, and biotech, on the other hand, tend not to pay any dividends because they are reinvesting most of their retained earnings back into their company for growth.

To achieve $10,000 in annual passive income at the S&P 500's 2% dividend yield, you would need to invest roughly $500,000. Or instead of investing in the S&P 500 index, you could invest $183,800 into AT&T stock given its 5.44% estimated dividend yield.

4) *Private Equity Investing*

Private equity investing can be a tremendous source of passive income with the right investments. If you find the next Uber, the returns will blow every single other passive income investment out of the water. But of course, finding the next Uber is a tough task since most private companies fail.

The most liquid of the private investments are investing in equity or credit hedge funds, real estate funds, and private company funds. There will usually be 6 month – 3 year lockup periods. The least liquid of the private investments are when you invest directly into private companies yourself. You might not be able to get your money out for 5-10 years, depending on the success of the company and upcoming liquidity events. Access to private investments are restricted to accredited investors, which is why the Feasibility Score is only a 4. But the Activity Score is a 10, because you can't do anything even if you wanted to. You're investing for the long term. The Risk and Return score greatly depends on your investing acumen and access.

Gaining $10,000 a year in private equity investing is difficult to quantify unless you are investing in a real estate or fixed income fund. Such funds generally target 8-15% annual returns, which equates to a need for $83,000 – $125,000 in capital.

5) Creating Your Own Products

If you're a creative person, you might be able to produce a product that's able to generate a steady flow of passive income for years to come. At the extreme, Michael Jackson, makes more dead than alive due to the royalties his estate makes from all the songs he produced in his career – an estimated $140 million in 2014 according to Forbes.

Of course it's unlikely any one of us will replicate the genius of Michael Jackson, but you could produce your own eBook, e-course, award-winning photo, designing and selling t-shirt with Teespring, affiliate marketing or articles online to create your own slice of passive income.

My esteemed marketing colleagues initially balked at the idea of creating products that generate royalties, so I can understand how creating something from nothing might be daunting for those who aren't even in creative roles. However, realize there is this enormous world out there of photographers, bloggers, artists, and podcasters who are making a passive income thanks to the Internet.

In 2012, even I wrote a 150-page eBook about severance package negotiations that still regularly sells about ~35 copies a month at $85 each (2nd edition for 2017) without any effort. In order to generate $2,975 a month or $35,700 a year in passive income as I do now, I would need to invest $892,500 in something that generates a 4% yield! To earn $10,000 a year in passive income would therefore need roughly $250,000 in capital.

Ask yourself how many hours a week do you spend sitting in silence, coming up with an idea and working on your idea?

We're so busy with our jobs that our childhood creativity sadly vanishes at some point in our lives. There are food bloggers who clear over $15,000 a month. There are lifestyle bloggers who make over $10,000 a month while living in Thailand. And there are even personal finance bloggers who've sold their sites for multi-millions.

Leveraging the internet to create, connect, and sell is something every creative person should attempt to do. The only risk is lost time and a wounded ego. You can start a site like mine for as little as $2.95 a month with Bluehost and go from there. They give you a free domain name for a year. Forget all the add-ons. Not a day goes by that I'm not grateful for my site.

I truly believe generating $10,000 a year online can be done by anybody who is willing to dedicate at least two years to their online endeavors. Here is a snapshot of what a real blogger makes through his website and because of his website. Roughly $150,000 a year is semi-passive income followed by another $186,000 a year in active income found through his site. Check out my guide on how to start your own blog here.

Warnings about Passive Income

Now that you know of some of the best sources of passive income, it's time to go over a few warnings. You'll want to know these, because if not, it could end up being disastrous for you if you undertake passive income. This chapter will go over some of the biggest warnings about passive income, and what you can do in order to prevent this in your life as well.

1) **You will have competition:** This is something that's especially big in the creative fields. You'll always have something or someone that is going to be there as competition. If you're not ready to see this, and act accordingly to whatever points to keep in the game, you'll definitely get the brunt of the results of this. Do keep in mind that you'll have competition, and to be successful, you'll need to get the results that you need fast, and try to keep ahead of the competition as best as you can.

2) **There are sudden changes:** don't just think that you can put it there and never think about it again, especially with home ownership and lending. There are changes that can suddenly happen, various things that can go wrong. If you're not ready to step in and make changes when it happens, you're going to need to think about another line of passive income. Now yes, there is less work with this, but remember that things happen, changes come about, so be ready.

3) **Handle people's gripes:** this goes with the second part of this, but if you passively leave things to go by themselves, you'll lose people. If you just passively let the complex run itself, it'll eventually lose the tenants at the end of the day, and maybe even you'll lose money. You need to still keep one foot in the door, and you should help those with complaints and issues. You can definitely

do this easily, and without a ton of time, but you'll want to keep this in mind.

4) **It's not as easy as you think:** this needs to be reiterated and put on a sign. Passive income isn't easy. You've got to work at it until it reaches the point of ease, and even then, you should check on it from time to time. By doing this, you'll actually have a steady income, and you'll be able to live your dreams, but remember that hard work is the answer to this.

5) **It's never always passive:** one thing that people forget is that it's not really passive. Again, this goes with what's said before, because often, people think that they can just run away once it's done. Sure, you can hire a property manager or team, and they can handle a lot of the dirty work, but are you really going to just up and abandon this? I doubt it, so remember that it's not always going to be a passive adventure, but rather, it does need some TLC every now and then, especially when you're looking to keep it going.

6) **Don't become passive-minded:** this is a big one that happens to those that generate a passive income. This happens to a lot of younger people who have some passive income before many things go down, or they start to realize the money well runs dry. Some of these people might be living the dream from this, but then, they kind of just forget and leave behind the business they've created.

This means that they've kind of given up on their passive dreams, and because of this, often the goal and purpose goes away. Sure, you're making a ton of money, but if you don't have a goal, you won't be happy. Simple as that. So when you are creating passive income, you've got to have that dream and idea still there, maybe even doing more of the same thing. Keep your mind strong and your brain working, and in truth, you'll have a more fulfilling and happier life.

7) **Doing nothing to get something:** this is a mindset that if you have it, you've got to do away with it now. You'll want to make sure you're doing something to get to this. Any of these little get-rich-quick schemes don't work, and in truth, you do need to cultivate all businesses. Think of them like a pet, something that needs to be looked at. Because if you just leave anything going without trying to do something about it, you might end up with a terrible situation, where you have rental properties that are falling apart. You definitely don't want to just leave things at that if you're not ready to work for it.

8) **Treat it as a business**: in essence, this is a mindset that you need to have. Do treat it as a business. You'll want to make sure that you do keep this as something that is there, especially if you're going in. If you stop considering this to be something that'll just magically come to fruition, you'll make more money.

9) **Not have fun:** if you're doing something without any element of fun attached, it can be hard. Passive income is the same way. If you hate doing real estate, you won't get results with this. You'll get people that obviously see you hate it, and in truth, it's definitely apparent. So keep that in mind, and when you choose something, you should make sure that you keep at it.

10) **You need to do your homework:** this is something that I can't stress enough, especially for those starting in a field that isn't like what they're used to, such as real estate or the like. Don't run into this thinking you know everything. Don't think after reading one book you can take on this huge rental property. You won't, you're going to fail. The same goes for investing. If you want to lose all of your money right away, then just walk in there blindly and without a care. Instead, take the time, do your

homework, and work towards your goal. You'll get way more and better results out of this.

Conclusion

I hope you learned how to use passive income in your life to the best of your abilities, and you'll be able to achieve your goals with it. For many people, this is something that doesn't seem realistic initially, but upon further inspection and engagement, it's totally possible. That's right, you can make passive income, and you just have to follow what it says here, and choose the right one for you.

That's indeed what your next step is. **Choosing the right passive income can make or break your adventure,** and often, this is the first step many take, and the one so many think about initially. But of course, by doing this effectively, you'll be able to achieve the various nuances and dreams that you have, and the goals that you've always wanted.

So what are you waiting for? Take the time, work on passive income, and from there, see what you can fully accomplish with this, and you'll be truly amazed by the certain aspects of this, and the dreams that you wish to achieve, and the possibilities that are out there that are both endless, and totally doable as well.

www.ingramcontent.com/pod-product-compliance
Lightning Source LLC
Chambersburg PA
CBHW030459220526
45464CB00006B/2573